LINWOOD

WORLD RELIGIONS

HINDUISM

Dilip Kadodwala

Wayland

First published in 1995 by
Wayland (Publishers) Ltd,
61 Western Road, Hove,
East Sussex BN3 1JD

This book was prepared for Wayland (Publishers) Ltd
by Ruth Nason

Book design: Alex Latham, Ken Alston

Typeset: A.J. Latham Ltd,
Houghton Regis, Dunstable, Bedfordshire

Printed and bound in Italy by G. Canale & C.S.p.A., Turin

British Library Cataloguing in Publication Data
Kadodwala, Dilip
    Hinduism. – (World Religions Series)
    I. Title. II. Series
    294.5

    ISBN 0–7502–1444–9

Cover: *Ringing the bell to
announce the start of
worship (John Smith,
Circa Photo Library).*
Page 1: *Hindu pilgrims at
Tirumala.*
Page 3: *The festival of
Holi, in the Hindu month
of Phalguna (February/
March), is enjoyed
especially by children, who
spray people with water
mixed with different-
coloured dyes.*

Acknowledgements

The author is grateful for the priestly support given by Shri
Jagdishbhai Bhatt in writing this book. Thanks also to my parents,
my wife Vilash and our sons Devan and Viren. This book is dedicated to them.

The author and publishers thank the following for their permission
to reproduce photographs: Circa Photo Library: pp. 8, 10, 17
(top), 24, 25, 35; Robert Harding Picture Library: p. 9; Hutchison
Library: p. 41 (Liba Taylor); Christine Osborne Pictures: pp. 6, 15
(top), 19, 22; TRIP: pp. 1 (F. Good), 3 (H. Rogers), 4 (top)
(P. Emmett), 4 (bottom) (B. Peerless), 5 (P. Emmett), 7 (top)
(B. Peerless), 7 (bottom) (R. Graham), 11 (Vitahalbai Collection,
Dinodia Press Agency), 12 (B. Turner), 13 (P. Rauter), 15
(bottom) (F. Good), 17 (bottom) (H. Rogers), 18 (P. Emmett), 20
(H. Rogers), 21 (P. Emmett), 23 (F. Good), 26, 27 (H. Rogers),
29 (P. Emmett), 30 (top) (P. Emmett), 30 (bottom) (H. Rogers),
31 (H. Rogers), 32 (P. Emmett), 33 (P. Emmett), 34 (H. Rogers),
37 (B. Turner), 38 (B. Peerless), 39 (P. Emmett), 42 (P. Emmett),
43 (P. Emmett), 44 (H. Rogers), 45 (top) (H. Rogers), 45
(bottom) (H. Rogers).

Contents

INTRODUCTION

The variety of ideas within the Hindu religion is like the variety of tastes in a traditional Indian vegetarian meal.

What does it mean to be a Hindu? You might expect the answer to be that a Hindu believes in the teachings of the person who founded the Hindu religion. But this answer would be wrong! Hinduism has no one single founder. Nor did the religion begin at any fixed point in history. Hinduism is certainly one of the oldest religions in the world, and most Hindus would agree that it is best understood as a rich and varied way of life.

The word 'Hindu' comes from the name of a river in northern India. About 3,500 years ago, people called the Aryans invaded the north-western part of India, and they called the river the 'Indus'. At first, the word 'Hindu' was used to mean these people, who lived beyond the Indus. Today the religion of Hindus is still closely connected with India, where the great majority of Hindus live.

'Hinduism' is a more modern word, first used by Europeans in the early nineteenth century. Hindus themselves do not always recognize or use the word to describe their religion. They prefer 'dharma' or 'Sanatan dharma', which means 'the eternal religion'. To be a Hindu means to be born into a tradition and a way of life, and to share certain beliefs and practices.

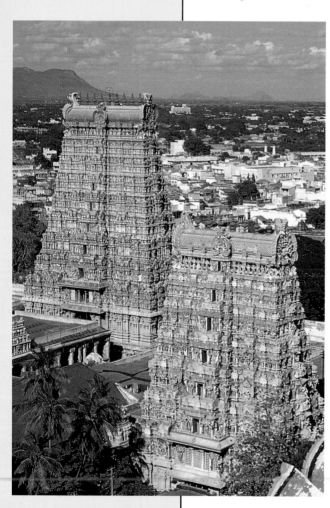

The gateway towers of the Meenakshi temple in Madurai, southern India, stand 48 metres high.

Imagine you are invited to a traditional Indian vegetarian meal. Usually it would be served as a 'thali', which means that the food is offered on one large circular stainless steel plate. On this plate would be a mix of spicy vegetables, rice, pulses and sweetmeats, each in a separate stainless steel bowl. You might also have some 'chappati' or 'nan' (types of bread) and a variety of chutneys. Now think of this thali as a symbol of Hinduism. Just as the food has a blend of ingredients and spices, so the religion has a variety of beliefs, and Hindus may approach them in varied ways.

These images of deities are on their way to be installed in a temple. It is a holy occasion, and so the images are adorned with regal clothes and garlands of flowers.

Central to the religion (the circular plate) is the Hindu idea of God. Hindus describe God as 'Brahman', which means the Supreme Being or Reality. Brahman has no form and is everywhere, in people, plants and animals. The spirit of Brahman in humans is 'atman'.

It is not always easy to think of God as formless, and so some Hindus use images of Brahman to help them worship. In this sense, Hindus believe that God can be worshipped in different forms. Hinduism therefore has thousands of gods and goddesses. Each represents some aspect of Brahman, and the vast number of them emphasizes the idea that Brahman is everywhere.

TRIMURTI

Hindus sometimes express their understanding of God as 'trimurti': three images. These are Brahma, the Creator, Vishnu, the Preserver, and Shiva, the Destroyer.

People believe that whenever there is an increase of evil in the world, the Supreme Being appears on earth, to defeat evil. These appearances are called 'avatars'. For example, Vishnu is believed to have appeared as nine different avatars, including Krishna and Rama.

DHARMA

'Dharma' has three meanings:

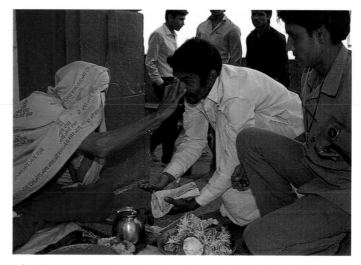

At the entrance of the Mahalakshmi temple in Bombay. A worshipper has a 'tilak' mark put on his forehead, before he goes inside to pray. Devout followers of Vishnu or Shiva have these markings, made with powders and ashes, to show their devotion to God.

🕉 religion.

🕉 the form of things as they are in the universe and the power that maintains them. For example, the dharma of fire is to burn.

🕉 one's personal duty – to behave righteously and to fulfil one's obligations towards family, society and God.

Two essential ingredients of the Hindu 'thali' are the beliefs about 'dharma' and 'karma'. Hindus say that each individual has his or her own dharma, meaning 'duty'. The idea of karma is that everything in the universe is subject to causes and effects. Individual good actions have good effects. If humans cause suffering to others, then they too will meet suffering.

This idea is linked to the Hindu belief that life is a cycle of birth, death and rebirth, called 'samsara'. One's next existence depends on how far one fulfils one's dharma by living correctly and performing good actions – good karma.

Hindus aim finally to be released from the repeated cycle of birth, death and rebirth. This release is called 'moksha'. Three things are necessary to achieve it: good actions, an understanding that the spirit of God (Brahman) and the spirit in humans (atman) are linked, and devotion to one's chosen god or goddess. Hindus sometimes refer to these three paths as 'karma yoga', 'jnana yoga' and 'bhakti yoga'. They and the teachings of the Hindu scriptures are also essential ingredients of the Hindu thali.

THE STORY OF
HINDUISM

This seal found at Mohenjo-daro is evidence that bulls were important in the beliefs of the people of the Indus Valley.

The Hindu religion is as old as Indian civilization, which can be traced back almost 5,000 years. A wide range of beliefs and practices have evolved over a very long period of time.

The Indus Valley, 3000-1700 BCE

Archaeologists in the twentieth century made an exciting discovery of the remains of an ancient civilization in the Indus Valley. Some of these remains were found at Mohenjo-daro and Harappa, in what is now called Pakistan. They showed that the people who lived here, from about 3000 to 1700 BCE (Before the Common Era – see page 47), had a highly developed lifestyle.

The great bath discovered at Mohenjo-daro is evidence that bathing was a part of religious practice for the Indus Valley people.

THE SWASTIKA

In Sanskrit the swastika sign means 'bringing health'. The arms represent paths to God. They are bent, because the paths are difficult. The arms all come from a central point and this shows how everything in the universe grows from a single source.

The symbol also represents the sun. This is why Hindus see the swastika as a sign of good fortune and protection against evil. It is used as a sign of God's blessing at a time of new beginnings. For example, the symbol is marked on a coconut, using 'kum kum' (red paste) during a wedding ceremony.

The archaeologists found figures and seals, which showed that people worshipped a mother goddess and a bull. Some of the figures are smoke-stained, perhaps because people kept a little lamp burning in front of them. It is also believed that the Indus Valley people practised religious rituals linked with bathing. Such practices are continued by Hindus today.

Archaeologists also found examples of the 'swastika' symbol in the Indus Valley. This is a cross with four arms of equal length, each one bent in the same direction. It is still an important symbol to Hindus today.

This decorated 'arti' tray (see page 34) won first prize in a competition held at the festival of Diwali.

The Aryan invasion

In about 1500 BCE a group of people called the Aryans invaded the north-western part of India, the area of the Indus Valley. These Aryans were linked with the land of Persia (now called Iran). Over time, more Aryans came and fought with the people who were the original settlers. They eventually conquered these people and some were driven further south.

The Vedic period, 1500-600 BCE

The Aryans worshipped deities (gods) associated with nature. Indra was the 'Lord of the Sky', Agni, the 'Lord of Fire' and Varuna, the 'Lord of the Waters'.

Their deities were male, but they adopted the worship of the mother goddess from the original inhabitants of the Indus Valley.

From about 1200 BCE the Aryans composed hymns, which were remembered and passed on by word of mouth. These became the earliest Hindu scriptures, called the 'Vedas'. The period of the Aryans in India is therefore called the 'Vedic period' and their religion is called the 'Vedic religion'.

The information we have about the religion comes from the Vedas. Instructions for fire sacrifices and the use of prayers also date from the Vedic period.

The Aryans organized their society according to occupations. One group was the priests or 'brahmins'. Some people began to challenge the special power which the priests had.

A brahmin priest today reads from some sacred texts and explains their meanings to a group of worshippers.

SANSKRIT

The Aryans spoke a language which was an early form of Sanskrit, the ancient Indian language in which the Hindu scriptures were later written.

Hindus regard Sanskrit as a sacred language, and many prayers are recited in this language today.

Early Hinduism, 600 BCE-200 CE

From about 600 BCE, criticism of the power of the priestly group or 'caste' led to the development of other religions, Jainism and Buddhism. This had an effect on the Vedic religion.

Some people now worked out detailed rules for general behaviour in life. The 'Manusmriti' ('Laws of Manu') set out the duties of each of four 'castes', or groups of society. These were the priests, rulers, merchants and craftsmen. Teaching also developed about a person's life consisting of four stages, with particular duties linked to each.

People paid less regard to the nature deities of the Vedic period and gave their devotion instead to the gods Vishnu and Shiva. Worship at home became more important than public worship, and the idea of showing love and devotion to a personal deity or god began to emerge.

Daily Hindu worship is often performed at home. Hindu homes have a shrine especially for this purpose.

During this time also the two epic scriptures, the 'Mahabharata' and the 'Ramayana' came into being.

The Puranic period, 300-1200 CE

Hindu practices as they are known today were fully developed between 300 and 1200 CE. This period is called 'the Puranic period', after some texts named the 'Puranas', which means 'ancient stories'. They contain some of the main Hindu myths and stories which influenced the religious beliefs and practices of ordinary people. A movement which encouraged all people to express devotion to a personal god began in southern India and gradually spread northwards. It is sometimes known as 'bhakti', or devotionalism.

Also during the Puranic period, gifted religious thinkers developed complicated Hindu philosophy. Two of these thinkers were Shankara and Ramanuja. People today still study their ideas about questions like 'How are humans related to God?'

Modern Hinduism

During the nineteenth and twentieth centuries reform movements have emerged and changes have been made, to try to keep the main Hindu beliefs and adapt them to changing circumstances. The need to adapt is particularly great for Hindus who now live away from India, in other parts of the world.

MAHATMA GANDHI (1869–1948)

In Gandhi's time, the British ruled India. Gandhi led a protest movement, for Indian independence. He insisted that the protesters should not use any violence and this idea was inspired by his belief, as a Hindu, that all life is sacred. Gandhi used the word 'ahimsa', which means more than just 'non-violence'. For him, it also meant expressing love and humility.

Hindus gave Gandhi the title 'Mahatma', which means 'great soul'. This was because, through actions in his life, he showed how love can defeat evil. Even as he lay dying, after a man had shot him, Gandhi forgave his killer. His example has inspired people in the West who have wanted to bring about changes for the better in their societies. For instance, in the 1960s, Martin Luther King led a movement, using non-violent methods, to champion the rights of black people in the USA.

The modern period has also seen the rise of sects such as the Swaminarayan Hindu Mission and the International Society for Krishna Consciousness, popularly known as the 'Hare Krishna' movement.

HARE KRISHNA

The Hare Krishna movement was founded by Bhaktivedanta Swami Prabhupada, who brought its ideas to the West in 1965. The ideas are based on the teachings of a saint called Chaitanya Mahaprabhu (1485-1533), who practised his love for God by worshipping Krishna. People who belong to this movement are strict vegetarians. Sometimes groups of them walk through the streets, chanting:

'Hare Krishna Hare Krishna Krishna Krishna Hare Hare
Hare Rama Hare Rama Rama Rama Hare Hare.'

'Hare' means 'God who forgives your wrong-doings'.

Followers of the Hare Krishna movement chanting and dancing in the streets of Vladivostok, Russia.

2
THE WORLD OF HINDUS

Of all religions, the Hindu religion has the third largest number of followers. It is closely associated with the land of India. In 1994, this vast country, which is larger than all of Western Europe, had a population of about 900 million. Around 83 per cent of these people are Hindus. India has sixteen main languages which the government has officially recognized and there are hundreds of regional dialects. It is hardly surprising that Hindu beliefs and practices vary from region to region.

The majority of Hindus live in India (and some in Pakistan), but there are also many in other countries. Their families have migrated from India over the past. Outside India and Pakistan, the greatest number of Hindus in one area are in East Africa. Large Hindu communities are also found in Nepal, Sri Lanka, South Africa, Bali in Indonesia, Surinam and Fiji.

Celebrating the festival of Diwali at Udaipur, India. 'Diwali' or 'Deepavali' means a 'row of lights'. Here the lights are floated on water.

THE MEHTA FAMILY

Geeta Mehta and her family moved from Bombay to New York, when she was ten. Five years later she says:

'We are vegetarians, because as Hindus we believe that all life is sacred and has to be respected. My father, who is a doctor, says that vegetarianism is good for health reasons too!

In Bombay it was easier to live as Hindus. There was always a fresh supply of many different vegetables and fruit. When we went out to eat, we did not have to ask if the food had been cooked in vegetable oil. I am pleased that some fast food places here use vegetable oil to make French fries.

Here, we have a family shrine where we pray every morning and evening. We also go to a temple, especially for Diwali. My parents tell me stories from the Ramayana. I like watching it on video too. My father buys a monthly Hindu family newspaper called *Hinduism Today*. It is good because it reminds me that we are Hindus and that there are many like us all over the world.'

In the past, some Hindus went to work in the West Indies, in places such as Trinidad and Tobago, and in Guyana. During the twentieth century, Hindus have also settled in Australia, Europe, Canada and the USA. Many of them trace their roots to India and East Africa. Families still keep regular contact with relatives in these countries and often visit them.

Holy places

For a devout Hindu, the entire land of India is sacred. It is believed that God has four dwelling places called 'dhams', at Badrinath in the north, Puri in the east, Rameshvaram in the south and Dwarka in the west. These places have important temples dedicated to Vishnu and Shiva. Some other temples in India are dedicated to the female aspect of God. One example is the Meenakshi temple, at Madurai (see page 4).

A temple dedicated to Shiva, at Kapalesawar, India.

At Puri the temple is dedicated to Jagannath, which is another name for Vishnu. During the annual festival of Rathayatra, a huge image of Jagannath is mounted on a giant chariot and pulled along the streets of Puri. The word 'juggernaut', in the English language, comes from the name of this deity.

Mountains and rivers are the other major holy sites. Some Hindus call the Himalayas the 'dwelling place of the gods'. Many journey to the mountains, such as Abu, as a way of purifying their body and mind and as a way of experiencing God.

Crowds at the Rathayatra festival.

Pilgrimage

Hindus from across India and other parts of the world go on pilgrimage to holy places. They may undertake journeys to visit their gurus (religious and spiritual teachers), or because they have made a special vow, or as a way of offering thanks to God. Others see their pilgrimage as a way of gaining merit, or good karma.

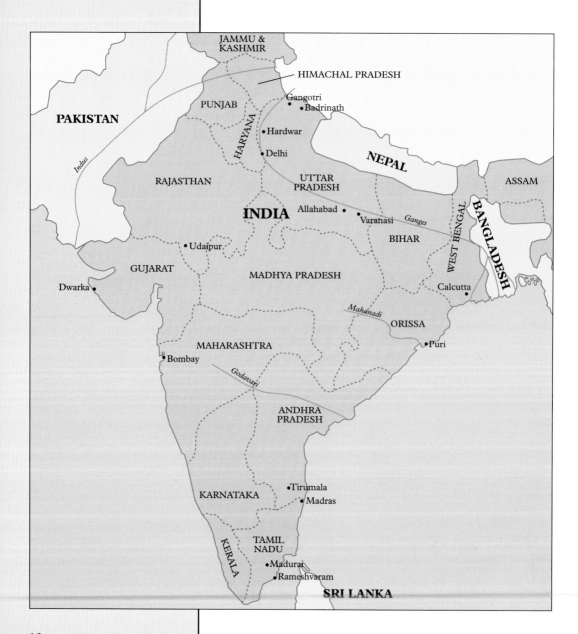

The holy city of Varanasi (Banares), on the banks of the River Ganges, is especially important to Hindu pilgrims.

The River Ganges

Hindus call this river the 'Ganga' and also describe it as 'the River of Heaven', because of the belief that it flowed in heaven before coming to earth. Pilgrims to the Himalayas climb to Gangotri, where the river first emerges from under a glacier.

The Ganges is often shown in art as flowing from Shiva's hair and down through the Himalayas. This figure of Shiva is from the door of the Shiva temple in Mombasa, Kenya.

A Hindu belief is that bathing in the Ganga cleanses away the bad karma of previous lives. Dawn is thought to be the best time for bathing, and at Varanasi, which is sometimes called 'Kashi' (City of Light), Hindus from all backgrounds bathe and perform worship.

Hardwar and the city of Allahabad, often called Prayag, are other special places on the Ganga. At Prayag, the rivers Ganges and Jumuna meet. A colourful festival called the 'kumbhamela' takes place here every twelve years. Millions of pilgrims attend.

Dawn worship at Varanasi. Many devout Hindus also express a wish to die at Varanasi, or, at least, to have their ashes scattered on the Ganga there. They believe that Varanasi is the crossing place between heaven and earth. Therefore to die here is to be freed from the cycle of rebirth.

3

SHASTRAS

Most Hindu scriptures are in the ancient Indian language called Sanskrit. The Sanskrit word for scriptures is 'shastras'. It means 'texts that explain and guide the way people behave in life'.

THE SCRIPTURES

Hindu scriptures, or 'shastras', have been divided into two groups. Some are called 'shruti', which means 'heard' or 'revealed' scriptures. This refers to wise men in ancient times who are believed to have heard God's word directly. The second group of scriptures is called 'smriti', which means 'remembered'. The scriptures were passed on orally for hundreds of years before they were written down.

The Vedas

The shruti texts include the four 'Vedas', which are some of the oldest Hindu scriptures. 'Vedas' means 'knowledge' or 'wisdom'. The first is the 'Rig-veda', which contains hymns praising the gods and goddesses of the Aryan people.

The four Vedas were composed between 1200 and 1000 BCE. Priests memorized them and passed them on by word of mouth. It was not until about 1400 CE that they were first written down.

Public readings from the sacred texts are often given, especially during festivals.

A PRAYER TO SAVITRI

The Rig-veda contains a prayer to Savitri, a sun god. Hindus recite this prayer every morning.

Om bhur bhuvah svahah
tatsavitur varenyam
bhargo devasya dhimahi
dhiyo yo nah prachodayat

This can be translated as:

We meditate on the loving light of the god, Savitri. May his brilliance, like that of the sun, stimulate our thoughts.

The prayer is also known as the Gayatri mantra. Hindu children are encouraged to learn it by heart.

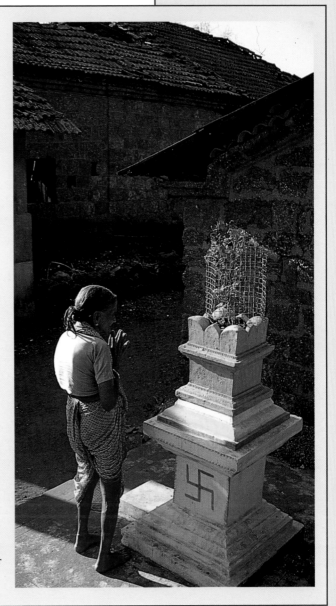

In some villages in India, a home shrine is outdoors, but still within the boundary of the home.

ॐ भूर्भुवः स्वः तत्सवितुर्वरेण्यं भर्गो देवस्य धीमहि धियो यो नः प्रचोदयात् ॥

The Gayatri mantra written in Sanskrit.

The Upanishads

Also among the shruti texts are scriptures called the 'Upanishads'. Literally, the word means 'near-down-sit'. Imagine a group of young men sitting down near their older teachers, called gurus, deep in the forests of northern India, at the foot of the Himalayas. They would be discussing ideas about the nature of the universe and why humans have been created. The beliefs that came out of these discussions, about Brahman, the Supreme Being, and atman, the human soul, were recorded in the Upanishads between 400 and 200 BCE.

There are 108 of these texts. The shortest consists of only eighteen verses, of two or four lines.

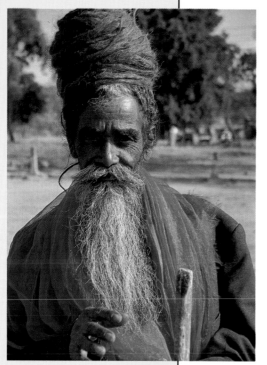

Holy men called 'sadhus' sometimes travel the length and breadth of India, visiting places regarded as especially holy. This sadhu is in Hardwar, a pilgrimage site in northern India.

THE BRIHADARANYAKA UPANISHAD

From the unreal
lead me to the real

From the darkness
lead me to light

From death
lead me to immortality.

These verses remind Hindus that, ultimately, only God is real. This does not mean that life on earth is not real, or that death is not real. But humans should not be fooled into thinking that life is all that there is and that there is nothing beyond. People who truly understand this achieve 'everlasting life'. This text is sometimes read during a death ceremony.

The Mahabharata

The ideas and experiences of wise men recorded in the shruti texts were not easy for most Hindus to understand. Therefore commentaries and stories were developed, to convey the spiritual truths contained in the texts and to make sure these were not lost. The stories were often acted out in the many villages of India.

The first of the stories, or epics, is called the 'Mahabharata'. It belongs to the smriti ('remembered') group of scriptures. The Mahabharata has 100,000 verses and includes the 'Bhagavad-gita', the 'Song of the Lord'.

The Bhagavad-gita

The Bhagavad-gita is the most respected of the Hindu scriptures. In it, Krishna, who is one of the avatars (forms) of Vishnu, the Preserver, reveals himself to his friend Arjun. He has come as God, in human form, to teach people how to overcome evil and to lead dutiful lives.

The Bhagavad-gita deals with some of the more difficult ideas discussed in the Upanishads, but in a way that all Hindus can understand. In it, Krishna explains, for example, how humans can overcome the cycle of birth, death and rebirth, particularly through loving devotion – 'bhakti' – towards him. The Bhagavad-gita has been translated into many Indian languages and also into English.

Stories about the lives of gods and goddesses are often explained through dance and drama. This dancer is performing a story about Krishna.

DEVOTION TO KRISHNA

When a Hindu offers gifts to God, he or she may remember this verse from the Bhagavad-gita. In it, Krishna is saying that the size of the offering is not as important as the love which the Hindu has in his or her heart.

pattram pusham phalam toyam
yo me bhaktya prayacchati,
tad aham bhakty-upahrtam
asnami prayat'atmanah.

Whoever offers to me a leaf,
a flower, a fruit or water with
    devotion,
that offering of devotion, I will
    accept
from the pure of heart.

Krishna is often portrayed blue and playing a flute. There are many stories of Krishna winning the hearts of cowgirls. This is another way of saying that God returns the love humans show for him.

The Ramayana

The second of the epic stories is called the 'Ramayana'. It consists of 24,000 verses and tells the story of the great god Rama and his wife Sita, who is captured by an evil demon. After a series of adventures, she is finally rescued. The story stresses the importance of faithfulness, love and truth and shows how good overcomes evil.

The Puranas

Other important scriptures are called the 'Puranas', which means 'ancient stories'. These also contain very long verses, relating Hindu myths. The stories told encourage Hindus to live dutiful lives.

HOME AND FAMILY LIFE

— 4 —

Children born into a Hindu family begin to learn about their religion at home. There is much that they can learn about Hindu beliefs and practices simply by living in a family and in a Hindu community.

Family relationships

In India, people live mostly in 'extended' families. Parents, children, grandparents and often aunts and uncles all live together, as part of one household. Grandparents play a large part in teaching the children about their religion.

In the West, Hindus do not always live in extended families. If they can, different branches of a family live close to one another, so that the children can benefit from the wisdom passed on across generations.

Many Hindus mark new beginnings, such as moving to a new home, with a religious ceremony.

TEN QUALITIES

It is the duty of grandparents and parents to teach that good behaviour is based on:

🕉 Telling the truth

🕉 Not stealing

🕉 Using intelligence to understand the difference between right and wrong

🕉 Developing knowledge about God

🕉 Being peaceful

🕉 Loving everybody

🕉 Being kind towards all creation

🕉 Behaving non-violently

🕉 Not having false attachments to worldly goods

🕉 Having faith in God

PUJA AT HOME

'When I wake up, I look at my hands. The fingers remind me of Lakshmi and the wrist reminds me of Saraswati. The palms remind me that God is ever-present in my life.

After my bath, I perform puja with my mother. She washes the murti (statue image) of Shiva and puts a small garland of flowers around it. She lights a ghee lamp and some incense, and then puts some kum kum paste on Shiva's forehead, using the fourth finger of her right hand. We have pictures of other gods and goddesses too and their foreheads are marked with kum kum. We also offer them sweets and fruit.

Next we do 'arti'. My mother moves a ghee lamp clockwise in front of the murti and the pictures, while we sing a prayer. We hold our hands over the lighted flame and then move them over our foreheads. This means we are receiving the blessings of Shiva.

My mother repeats the holy names of God, running her fingers through a 'mala' of 108 wooden beads. Finally, we share the food we have offered to the gods, so that we feel blessed and ready to face the day ahead.' (Usha, aged eleven, from Delhi, India)

Circling the arti tray in front of a murti.

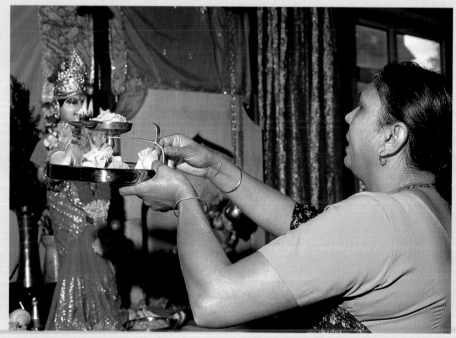

Worship at home

Every home has a shrine, where women in particular perform 'puja' (worship) every day. Worship can be long or short and can involve all the members of a family, including men. It takes place in the morning and evening, although in the West, some Hindu families choose to worship in the evening only, if the adults have to set off to work very early.

Washing murtis with milk and water.

KATHA

'Three or four times a year we have a 'katha', a religious gathering, at home. Twenty to thirty people attend, so we clear the furniture from the shrine room and everyone sits on the floor. A brahmin priest begins by performing puja. The sweet-smelling incense gives the feeling that God is present with us.

After the puja the priest chooses a story from his books. He tells the story without really looking at the book, and explains the difficult parts – sometimes in English! The story is usually about people or families who have had experiences of God.

One story I remember is about a man who lived a bad life, stealing and lying. Then, one day, he was passing through a village where a katha was taking place. He stopped to listen and this event changed his life completely. Stories like this are reminders to Hindus that God is everywhere. Treating all other people as if God is in them is another way of worshipping God.

After the story, we sing 'bhajans' (hymns) and finish by sharing the food ('prashad') that the priest has offered to God.'
(Bharat, aged twelve, from London)

Duties through life

Hindus see life as consisting of four stages – the 'brahmacharya' (student) stage, the 'grihastha' (householder) stage, the 'vanaprastha' (retirement) stage, and the 'saanyas' (renunciation) stage.

Hindus also have four aims in life – to do their duty (dharma), to make wealth ('artha') to help others, to fulfil their ambitions ('kama') but not to become attached to their success, and to gain release (moksha) from the cycle of rebirth.

Depending on which stage of life a person is in, one or some of these aims are seen as the most important.

For example, Hindus in the first, brahmacharya stage of life are encouraged to learn scriptures and to be educated so that they may earn a living. Children learn to respect their elders, as part of performing their duties.

In the villages of India, especially, people make patterns from coloured rice-flour on their doorsteps. These patterns are a way of welcoming God to the home. During the festival of Diwali, competitions for designing patterns are often held.

At the grihastha stage, men and women are expected to marry and have children and to contribute to the well-being of the community and of society. Part of the duties of a householder is to look after family members, including the elderly. Also a householder should contribute.to charities and help others by doing community work.

The 'vanaprastha' stage begins at about the age of fifty, when a person has probably fulfilled the desire to bring up a family and no longer needs to be so concerned about making money. The scriptures recommend that, at this stage, a person should begin to devote more time to spiritual matters. The person now

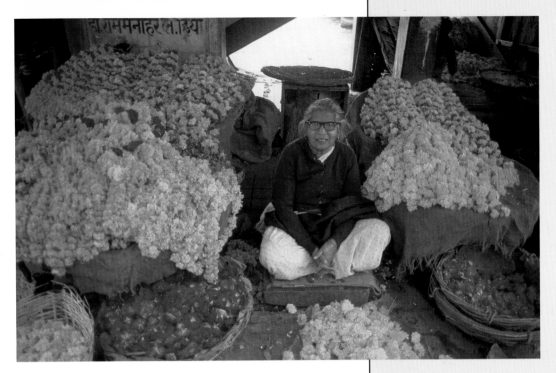

goes more often to the 'mandir' (temple) and to 'satsangs' (gatherings where scriptures, stories and songs are recited), often held in Hindu homes.

At the 'sannyas' stage, a person is supposed to give up all attachment to the material world and become a wandering monk. This gives the person time to concentrate on achieving 'moksha', final release from the cycle of birth, death and rebirth.

The aims given for the four stages of life set out broadly what a Hindu should try to achieve during the course of a lifetime. In practice, people do not fit rigidly into this pattern. Not all Hindus become forest dwellers at the fourth stage of life, for example! For Hindus living in the West, it is more difficult to divide life into the four stages. Generally, however, the four stages give a framework within which Hindus can practise their religion and fulfil their duties.

A person who carries out all his or her religious and moral duties according to his age, caste, occupation and financial means, is said to be being true to his or her 'dharma'.

Selling flowers outside a temple in Hardwar. Flowers are offered to God during worship. Also, in India, a way of greeting special guests and holy people is to place a garland of flowers around their necks.

27

VARNAS AND CASTES

The dividing of Indian society into groups goes back to ancient times. The Rig-veda describes four 'varnas': 'brahmin' (e.g. priests), 'kshatriya' (e.g. rulers), 'vaishya' (e.g. merchants) and 'shudra' (e.g. craftsmen). Each group had particular duties. The idea was that if each group fulfilled its duties, society would work well.

Later, varnas became incorrectly mixed with 'castes', and this caused problems. Castes or 'jatis' were smaller groups, often linked to occupations. People were not allowed to marry outside their group, and castes seen as the lower ones were treated badly.

In modern India, the traditions of caste are less strictly observed.

Belonging to a group

Hindus everywhere attach importance to the group of society, called the 'jati', into which they are born. Originally, each jati was linked to an occupation and members of the jati all followed that occupation. Nowadays people have more educational opportunities than in the past and it is common to move to find work, and so members of a jati can get jobs quite different from the traditional occupation of their group. This is especially the case in the West and in Indian cities. In the villages of India there has been less change. A person's jati can affect where he or she can live, and whom he or she can mix with. It is still usual for Hindus, including those in the West, to marry someone from their own group.

BELONGING TO A JATI

'We belong to the 'mochi' (shoemakers) jati. My grandfather was a shoemaker in Gujarat, India. He felt that education was very important and encouraged my father to study hard. Now my father is a pharmacist working in a London hospital and my grandfather is very proud of him.

We have a hall we can use, which was bought by our jati association with money given by other mochis. I go to classes there on Saturday mornings to learn to read and write Gujarati. We speak that language at home. The jati association also holds dances and festival celebrations at the hall. I like meeting other mochi families, especially other children who were born in England. It feels good to belong!'

(Harish Chudsana, aged fourteen, Birmingham, England)

————— 5 —————

COMMUNITY LIFE

Hindus come together at a mandir (temple) to perform puja (worship) and to keep links with other Hindus strong. In the West, Hindus also meet at the mandir to discuss community matters, and they hold events there to raise money to help others. Many mandirs have halls, where weddings take place, and rooms for classes, at which children learn languages and more about their religion.

Mandirs

There are thousands of mandirs in India. Some are huge, with beautiful and complicated designs inside and out. There are also tiny shrines alongside roads and in villages. This expresses again the idea that Brahman, the Supreme Being, is everywhere and is revealed in many forms.

A small mandir in India, with an image of the deity Hanuman above the central door and one of Ganesh on the right.

Inside a mandir. The alcove at the back is empty, waiting for the murtis (images, shown on page 5) to be installed.

Hindus believe that a mandir is a house where a deity or deities live. Each mandir is dedicated to Vishnu, Shiva or Shakti, the mother goddess. However, some temples house all three deities plus others, such as Ganesh and Hanuman. The main shrine in the temple has the image or 'murti' of the deity to whom the temple is dedicated. Surrounding shrines hold the murtis of the other deities.

Particular animals are associated with some deities. Images of these, and symbols and objects connected with the deities, may also be found in the temple.

In the West a mandir is usually a converted house or church. However, there are now purpose-built temples in some major cities where Hindu communities have become more settled.

A well-known image of Shiva is in the form of a dancer called Natraja. The circle of flames represents the destruction and re-creation of the universe.

Gods and goddesses

All the gods and goddesses of Hinduism are images of different aspects of Brahman, the one Supreme Being who has no form and is everywhere.

Most Hindus worship Vishnu, the Preserver, or Shiva, the Destroyer. It is possible to worship both of these deities, even though they seem contradictory. They represent opposite forces, which balance each other in life. Although Shiva is 'the Destroyer', he also has a creative aspect. He destroys and then re-creates the world. Shiva's creative side reveals itself as energy, which takes shape as the goddesses Kali or Durga. The energy is both creative and destructive, and so the goddesses are both gentle and terrible.

Both Vishnu and Shiva appear in many forms. Shiva is sometimes pictured as a householder who has a wife, the goddess Parvati. Their son is called Ganesh and their daughters are Lakshmi, the goddess of wealth and prosperity, and Saraswati, the goddess of knowledge and learning.

Some deities are portrayed with multiple faces and arms. Brahma, the creator of the universe, has four faces so that he can look in every direction at once. This is also a way of saying that God is everywhere. Brahma's four arms symbolize the points of the compass.

Most Hindu gods and goddesses have animals as their vehicles. The animals also represent some quality of the deity. A powerful bull called Nandi is usually linked with Shiva.

ANIMALS

Animals are believed to support the powers of the deities. Shiva's animal is a bull called Nandi. The goddess Parvati rides a tiger. Pictures like this show the deities' mastery over powerful animals. Shiva also wears a five-headed cobra, usually over his head.

Brahma's hands carry symbolic objects: a water jug, as water is the source of life; a spoon, symbolizing offerings made during worship; prayer beads, a symbol of time; and a lotus flower, representing the universe, humanity and purity. Brahma's vehicle is a goose, which symbolizes wisdom.

Vishnu is shown with a sky-blue skin. Like the sky, he is everywhere and everlasting. In his four hands he carries a lotus, a conch-shell, a club and a wheel called 'chakra'. This symbolizes the circle of time, creation and death.

Worship

Hindus perform daily worship at home, so they are not expected to go to the mandir every day. Puja in the mandir takes place in the evening, although in some temples in India it takes place throughout the day. Every mandir has at least one person called a 'pujari', who leads the worship. A Hindu priest who conducts worship and also acts as a religious adviser has the title 'pandit'.

Ganesh is a popular Hindu deity. His pot belly symbolizes the universe and his elephant head represents his power to remove obstacles.

Worship follows a similar pattern at home and in a mandir. Before starting puja, worshippers bathe. In India, Hindus living near the Ganges immerse themselves in the river.

In the mandir, the pujari washes the murtis in water or milk. The images of the deities are treated as if they were honoured guests or royalty. Next the pujari anoints the murtis with sandalwood or turmeric or kum kum. A pujari has a 'tilak' mark on his forehead, made with these powders, and he makes a similar tilak mark on the murtis. He dresses the murtis in red and gold clothes and puts garlands of flowers on them. He offers food to them, usually in the form of fruit, and uses incense to purify and sweeten the air around them.

The worshippers do not see these preparations being made. The pujari performs all these rituals behind curtains. As he prepares, he chants short sacred texts called 'mantras' and recites prayers, in Sanskrit. Finally, before the curtains are drawn back so that the deities can receive the worshippers' praise, the pujari lights the 'arti' lamp or 'diva'. When the curtains are drawn back, the worshippers can 'see' and, it is believed, are 'seen' by God. Hindus call this special moment 'darshan'.

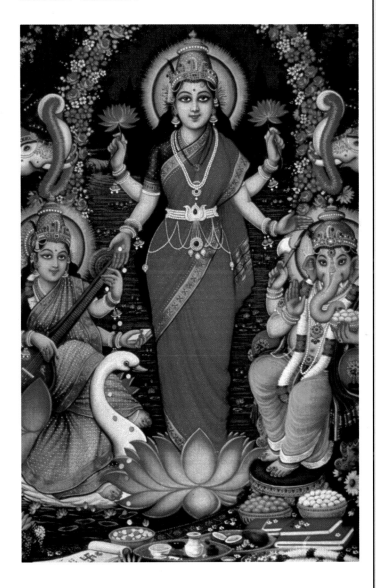

A conch-shell is often linked with Vishnu and his avatar Krishna, because it symbolizes a demon that Krishna destroyed. It reminds Krishna's devotees to destroy evil and ignorance in their lives. In a mandir, the conch-shell is blown to announce the start of worship.

A bell is used for a similar purpose. The bell ringing reminds the worshipper that he or she must try to concentrate on puja and drive away bad thoughts.

Lakshmi, the goddess of prosperity and good fortune, is often shown standing on a lotus flower. The goddess Saraswati is sometimes pictured riding a white goose.

ARTI

'Arti' is the offering of five lighted lamps, made by dipping cotton wool wicks in clarified butter called 'ghee'. The number five represents the five elements of nature, which are essential for human survival – water, fire, earth (including its products, such as fruit and flowers), air and space. Also the number five represents the five human senses. The idea is that people use all five senses in worship and so express their love, 'bhakti', for God with their whole being.

An arti lamp in the form of the Om symbol.

Now the pujari performs the arti ceremony. On behalf of the worshippers he places the five lamps in a steel tray, and moves the tray in a circle in front of the image of the main deity. This circling is done clockwise, from the top to the bottom of the murti. The tray is then moved from left to right to left again to make another circle. While this is happening, the worshippers sing a special hymn and chant a prayer. The singing is accompanied by music played on a harmonium, drums and cymbals. It ends with the worshippers' request to God: 'Bless me with ever-increasing faith, divine love and spirit of service.'

The pujari then circles the arti tray to the other three sides of the mandir. He sprinkles water, held in a conch-shell, over the worshippers, as a way of sharing God's blessings. As the worshippers sit down, they continue to share the blessings by passing the arti tray around. They put an offering of money in the tray and pass their hands over the lamps and then over their eyes as a sign of receiving God's blessings. As the worshippers leave the mandir, they take food blessed by God. This 'prashad' is made of nuts, fruit and sweets.

The sacred 'Om'

An important Hindu symbol is the sacred syllable 'Om', sometimes spelt as 'AUM'. This represents the sound of God. It is also the origin of all sound. The three letters are linked with Brahma, Vishnu and Shiva – with birth, life and death. This syllable is recited at the beginning and ending of prayers and when bhajans (hymns) or mantras (holy chants) are sung. The Mandukya Upanishad opens with the words: 'Everything is AUM. The past, present and the future and that which is outside time. Everything is AUM.'

6

A HINDU LIFETIME

The most important aim in life for a Hindu is to achieve release (moksha) from the cycle of birth, death and rebirth. To achieve moksha, a Hindu has to develop self-control and must not become attached to successes in his or her present life. By following the requirements of dharma (see pages 6 and 26), a person can gain good merits and so stand a better chance of achieving moksha.

The scriptures recommend sixteen steps to help achieve the goal of moksha. These steps are called 'samskars', or life cycle rituals or sacraments. Eleven of the rituals are performed during the first stage of life. They begin even before a baby is born. The sixteenth step takes place after a person has died.

An expectant Hindu mother, reciting prayers for a healthy child.

Birth

Some ceremonies are performed to ensure the well-being of the mother-to-be and her baby during pregnancy. Customs vary, depending on the jati people belong to and on where they live. A ceremony that is common to everyone occurs halfway through or towards the end of pregnancy. People recite prayers for a healthy child. The ceremony is followed by a feast for family members.

NAMES

Some boys' names linked to names of gods are Mahesh, Jagdish and Niranjan.

Girls' first names include Avni, which means 'earth', Padma, which is a name for a flower, and Usha, meaning 'dawn'. The girls' names Parvati, Savita and Ansuya are linked to names of goddesses.

Another ceremony is performed on the day of a baby's birth. In the presence of a Hindu priest, the father takes a gold ornament, such as a ring, dips it in a mixture of ghee (clarified butter) and honey, and holds it to the baby's lips. The father or the priest recites: 'May your life be as precious as gold. This will depend on your good thoughts, speech, deeds and behaviour.'

The father or priest then whispers in the baby's right ear: 'May God the creator of all things grant you firm wisdom. Knowledge and wisdom are the source of power and long life.' Family members, particularly grandparents, then bless the baby.

Naming a baby

The step of naming a child is taken on the twelfth day after birth. After a baby is born, the family asks a priest about names. The priest consults an almanac (a book giving information about each day in the year) and produces some syllables that can be used in the name. Some names have meanings associated with gods and goddesses or with the powers of nature.

In Gujarati Hindu families, the father's sister is given the honour of choosing the name.

The first outing

The baby is not taken outdoors for the first five weeks of his or her life. The scriptures recommend that the fourth month after birth is the ideal time for taking a baby outside for the first time. However, especially in the West, Hindu families find this idea difficult to follow. In ancient times, it was perhaps a way of ensuring that the child was protected from extreme weather conditions and from infectious diseases. On the baby's first outing, he or she is taken to a mandir to be blessed by God.

The first hair-cut

The eighth step, the first hair-cut or 'mundan', applies to male children, although a hair-cutting ceremony for girls is not unheard-of. The ceremony takes place at the age of one, or before the age of three or five. Until then, the hair is left uncut.

Hindus believe that the hair-cutting ceremony is a way of making sure that the karma of the child's previous life, as well as impurities collected in the process of being born, are 'washed away'. Some Hindu families, especially in India, put the hair in flowing water, for example in the Ganges. At the hair-cutting ceremony the parents express their wish that the child will be blessed with a fresh start in this new life.

After a hair-cutting ceremony.

ASHOK'S HAIR-SHAVING

Ashok had his hair-shaving ceremony at the age of five. It would have been sooner, but had to be delayed because his aunt died. A Hindu belief is that a year must go by after a death in the family, before a ceremony such as the first hair-cut is held. Ashok had had to put up with being mistaken for a girl!

A Hindu priest was invited to perform a sacred fire ritual before the hair-cutting. Afterwards, Ashok sat, rather fidgety, in his father's lap and the barber began to shave off all Ashok's hair. He used an electric shaver, which probably made the experience less unsettling than if he had used a razor, as in ancient times.

A little cool yogurt was put on Ashok's bare skull. Hindus regard yogurt as a pure substance, as it is made from milk. Then Ashok was bathed and his head was covered with a turban-shaped hat.

The sacred thread ceremony

The tenth of the sixteen steps is the sacred thread ceremony or 'upanayana'. It is for boys who belong to the first three castes. The scriptures recommend that for boys in the brahmin caste the ceremony should take place in their eighth year; for boys in the kshatriya caste, in their eleventh year; and for those in the vaishya caste, in their twelfth year. Not all Hindu families in these three castes have this ceremony performed. Some may leave it until the men are in their early twenties.

When the ceremony is performed in the earlier years, it also marks the boy's coming of age. It marks a time when a boy has begun to understand the meaning of belonging to a Hindu community. It also marks the beginning of his formal religious education.

This ceremony is both religious and social. It is performed in front of family and friends. A priest conducts a sacred fire ritual, called 'homa', and then places a loop of white cotton thread, made from three strands, over the boy's left shoulder, so that it hangs diagonally across his chest and under his right arm. The boy makes a vow to remain celibate until marriage and to fulfil his duties towards God, his parents and his religious teacher. After the ceremony there is a meal, to celebrate, and the boy receives presents.

A Hindu wedding

A Hindu sees marriage as holy, as it is the twelfth of the sixteen steps. Marriage is not only a union between two partners, but also an alliance of two families. In the past, the choosing of partners was left entirely to parents. It was their duty to 'arrange' a match, taking into account the caste and social positions and the future happiness of the proposed couple and their off-spring. Now young people are increasingly involved in choosing their own partners. These days a Hindu marriage is 'guided' rather than 'arranged'.

Once the choice is made, a priest looks up the partners' horoscopes to find a good time for the wedding. The bride's family arranges and pays for the use of a hall or mandir and provides a feast. Relatives may travel great distances to attend.

At the ceremony, the priest performs several rituals. Depending on the wishes of the families, a ceremony can last for up to six hours. The sacred fire or 'homa' is important. It is lit in a square metal or brick structure called a 'yajna-kund'. The priest invites the groom to drop ghee and grains (symbols of fertility) into the fire and, as he does so, the bride, seated on his left, touches him on the right shoulder with her right hand. They both walk round the fire, holding hands, and the husband says: 'Let us love and admire one another and protect each other. Let us see, hear and live a hundred autumns.'

They offer prayers for a long and happy life and for God's blessings for children. Some elements used during the ceremony, such as coconuts and rice, also represent fertility and the hope for healthy children.

A highlight of the wedding ceremony is when the couple take seven steps. The bride follows the groom, who says to her as they walk:

Take the first step for food.

Take the second step for power.

Take the third step for prosperity.

Take the fourth step for happiness.

Take the fifth step for children.

Take the sixth step for the enjoyment of pleasures.

Take the seventh step for lifelong friendship.

Taking the seven steps.

It is written in the Bhagavad-gita:
'Just as a man casts out worn-out clothes and puts on new ones, so also the embodied Self casts out worn-out bodies and enters others that are new.'

Hindus believe that where a human being is reborn and in what form depend on good and bad deeds gathered through life. Of course, the family and friends of the one who has died hope that she or he will not be reborn at all, but will achieve release from the cycle of rebirth.

Death and funerals

When someone dies, Hindus freely express their sorrow. Family, friends and neighbours give support. Comfort is also found in Hindu beliefs about life after death.

Hindu bodies are cremated (burned), not buried. At the cremation, the last of the sixteen life-cycle rituals is performed.

In India it is usual for a funeral pyre to be built near a river. If the person who has died is a man, close male relatives bathe his body and dress him in new clothes. Female relatives do the same if the dead person is a woman. Apart from wood, saffron, musk, sandalwood and camphor are used to make the funeral pyre. The eldest son or a close male relative lights the fire. A priest recites mantras (verses) in Sanskrit. When the body is reduced to ashes, they and the few bones which remain are collected and cast into a river. This is preferably the Ganges, because it is regarded as holy.

In the West, a funeral ceremony takes place at a crematorium, without a funeral pyre. Prayers and mantras are recited as in India. If possible, the family scatters the ashes in running water. More and more families now send the ashes to India, where they are scattered on the Ganges. Others make a special journey to scatter the ashes there themselves.

After the funeral, in some families, it is customary to eat some simple but especially prepared food, such as rice. The belief is that, if many people eat this food, there is a greater chance that the dead person's soul will find peace.

Fourteen days after the funeral, the family holds a feast. After this, they have an annual ceremony, as a way of remembering the person who died.

7

FESTIVALS

For Hindus, time is not like a straight line, with a beginning and an end, but more like the turning of a wheel. Time is cyclical and it is divided into four ages called 'yugas'.

Hindu months are based on the waxing and waning of the moon. Each month of thirty days has a 'light' fortnight leading up to the full moon and a 'dark' fortnight ending with the new moon. Because the calendar is lunar, the Hindu year is shorter than a year on the Western calendar. Festivals fall at changing times in the Western year and Hindus in the West use a calendar called a 'pattra' to keep track of festival dates.

Twelve lunar months make a Hindu year. However, that is counted as only one day in a 'gods' year'. There are 360 Hindu years in one 'gods' year', and 12,000 gods' years make up a cycle of four ages or yugas.

We are now in the worst age, which began with a battle described in the Mahabharata. On the Western calendar this took place in 3102 BCE. Hindus believe that when this yuga ends, Kalki, the tenth avatar of Vishnu, will descend to earth to begin a new, perfect age.

Raksha Bandhan
This festival takes place on the full-moon day of the Hindu month of Shravan (July/August). In north India it marks the start of the agricultural year. In western India it is a feast day and a public holiday. 'Raksha' means 'protection' and 'bandhan' means 'to tie'. On this day, Hindus tie a silk thread with a bauble, as shown above, on the wrist of friends and relatives.

In many families Raksha Bandhan is celebrated as a sisters' day. The 'tie of protection' ceremony begins with the sister putting a mark on the forehead of her brother, using kum kum. Then she ties the thread or 'rakhi' on her brother's right wrist, saying: 'May all your ambitions be fulfilled.' She offers him a blessing and a milk sweet, called 'barfi'. He gives her a present and makes a promise to protect her throughout her life.

The rakhi is a symbol for protection from evil and also for the strengthening of affection between sisters and brothers. Where a girl has no brother, male cousins are regarded as brothers. The ceremony then serves also as a reminder of the importance of family unity.

Krishnajanmashtami

This festival marks the birth of Krishna. It occurs on the eighth day of the dark half of Shravan. People fast until midnight. In homes and temples, they read from the scriptures and sing devotional songs. They adorn murtis of Krishna and his companion, Radha, and place gifts of milk sweets, fruit, leaves and flowers at their feet.

At the festival to mark the birth of Krishna, a cradle holding an image of Krishna as a baby is displayed in mandirs. Parents bring their children to this murti, to be blessed by Krishna.

At midnight, puja and arti ceremonies are performed. The fast is broken by sharing the food or 'prashad' blessed by God. Often a murti of Krishna as a baby in a cradle is revealed at midnight, and parents bring their children to the murti to be blessed.

Mahashivratri

'Mahashivratri' means the 'Great Night of Shiva'. Many Hindus fast every Monday as a mark of devotion to Shiva. On Mahashivratri, on the fourteenth day of the dark fortnight of Magha (January/February), the whole family may fast. Many families do not eat cooked meals but only fruit, nuts and barfi.

Navratri, Durgapuja and Dassehra

Navratri, which means 'nine nights', occurs after the monsoon rains, during the first ten days of the light half of the month of Ashvina (September/October). One of the few Hindu festivals celebrated all over India, it is also popular in the West. In India it has different names in different places. It is called Navratri in Gujarat in western India, Durgapuja in Bengal in eastern India, and Dassehra in northern India. Some of the celebrations differ too.

In Gujarat, India, and in the West, the festival of Navratri is marked by traditional dancing for nine nights.

Navratri is an important Gujarati Hindu festival which is also celebrated in Britain. It is dedicated to the worship of the mother goddess, in one or many of her forms. Ambaji is one of her names. A general term, 'mataji', meaning 'honoured mother', is also used.

The celebrations include dancing around a special shrine, made from a box with a cone-shaped top. There is a picture of the mother goddess in one of her forms on each side. There are two traditional dances: 'garba', a circle dance, and 'dandya ras', a stick dance. The dancing and devotional singing begin in the evening and continue well into the night. Hindus of all ages attend, some for the whole period of nine nights. It is a time for renewing friendships and strengthening community bonds.

FASTING

Men, women and older children fast at some festivals and at other times. Women may fast on a regular basis, as part of their duties. Some eat only once on the eleventh day of each fortnight. This fast is called 'agiaras'.

Many Hindus regard Shravan as a holy month. In this month, they eat only once a day, usually after sunset. Brahmin families, in particular, fast on Mondays of this month and break their fast after sunset. Devout Hindus avoid spicy foods and alcohol. Many men, mostly from brahmin families, do not shave during Shravan. In these ways Hindus practise self-discipline, learn to control desires, and show devotion to God.

In northern India the festival of Dassehra is connected with the story of Rama. Giant puppets of the main characters are made. Parts of the story are acted out, including the scenes leading to Rama's fight with the ten-headed demon Ravana. On the tenth day, the triumph of good over evil is marked by burning the puppet of Ravana, stuffed with fireworks, on a huge bonfire.

The nights are noisy, bright with colourful clothes and decorations, and full of energy. The goddess represents 'shakti' or energy and power. Hindus believe that the goddess's energy lives in them. They awaken it by taking part in the festival and it can then be used to overcome the evil which they meet in daily life. At the end of each night, the arti ceremony is performed and prashad is shared.

The goddess Durga is worshipped at the festival of Durgapuja in Bengal. This also lasts for nine nights and on the tenth day the festival murtis of Durga are carried to the river and immersed in the water. This is a way of saying that it is not the image that is important, but the deity herself. Another meaning is that the water carries away the bad things of life.

Diwali

Diwali is the most important Hindu festival and the main one celebrated in the West. The word is a shortened version of 'Deepavali', which means 'a row of lights'. The festival differs from place to place but in most cases people clean their homes and decorate them with garlands of flowers and paper chains. They light oil lamps. They wear new clothes and feast with relatives and friends.

The message of Diwali is that good overcomes evil; light can triumph over darkness. For many Hindus,

THE STORY OF RAMA AND SITA

Prince Rama and his wife Sita lived in the kingdom of Ayodhya in India. Through no fault of his, Rama was denied his place on the throne when his father the king died. He was banished to a forest for fourteen years, with Sita and his half-brother, Lakshmana. In the forest, Sita was captured by the king of demons, Ravana. He imprisoned her on the island of Lanka (now Sri Lanka).

After many battles and much struggle, Rama, helped by the forest animals and especially the monkey deity Hanuman, defeated Ravana and rescued Sita. Rama and Sita returned to Ayodhya, where Rama became king. For many Hindus, Diwali celebrates this return.

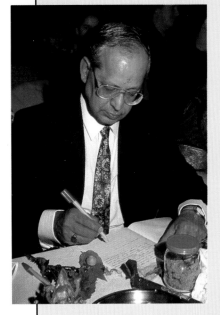

On the third day of Diwali Hindu people in business close their account books and offer worship to Lakshmi, praying for prosperity. In the West this ceremony is often held in a mandir, which gets very crowded.

Diwali celebrates the story of Rama and Sita and their return to their kingdom in India. Other stories linked with the festival are a tale of how Krishna defeated a demon called Naraka, and a story of King Bali's generous spirit.

Another part of Diwali is the worship of the goddess Lakshmi, who represents wealth as well as grace. On the third day, the house and surrounding areas are lit with oil lamps. Especially in Indian villages, people keep their doors and windows open. This is an invitation to Lakshmi to enter and bless the household.

Diwali is also a time for exchanging and sharing sweet food.

The fourth day of the festival is considered the most auspicious. A married woman receives a present from her husband, and children wear new clothes. It is a day for new beginnings and it resembles the marking of a New Year in other world customs.

Glossary

To show how words are pronounced, some stress marks have been added to the words in this Glossary.

'a' sounds like the 'a' in 'human'.
'ā' sounds like the 'a' in 'car'.
'i' sounds like the 'i' in 'sit'.
'ī' sounds like the 'ee' in 'meet'.
'u' sounds like the 'u' in 'bull'.
'ū' sounds like the 'oo' in 'soon'.

agiaras	word used mostly by Gujarati Hindus. It refers to the eleventh day of each half of the lunar month, when many Hindus fast.
ahimsā	not killing; non-violence – linked with respect for all forms of life.
ārti	an act of worship in which a cotton wick or wicks, dipped in clarified butter, are lit in front of an image of a deity and moved in a circle to show reverence.
ātman	self or soul in individuals; a spark of God in humans.
avatār	'descent to earth'; an incarnation of God on earth, to destroy evil.
bhajan	devotional song or hymn, sometimes chanted to music.
bhakti	devotion to God.
brahmin	member of a priestly group, the first of the four varnas.
chakra	wheel with thirty-two spokes. It has been adopted as India's national symbol.
dharma	can mean duty or conduct, right living, correct actions, and also religion.
dīvā	a twisted raw-cotton wick dipped in clarified butter and placed in a lamp made of earthenware or brass.
fast	a type of self-sacrifice which can mean not eating or drinking at all; or drinking only water and milk; or eating only certain foods, such as fruits.
ghee	melted butter which is clarified.
gurū	a religious teacher or guide, who helps to remove ignorance in the world.
homa	a fire ritual, mainly performed at weddings, during which offerings of wood, ghee and grains are made to the god of fire, Agni.
jāti	the social group to which a Hindu belongs by birth. Usually linked to an occupation.
karma	the belief that all actions have their effects, good and bad. A person's actions determine his or her future in this life and the next.
kathā	a gathering at which religious stories are told and explained by a priest.
kum kum	a red or saffron-coloured powder, made into a paste and used to anoint a deity.
mala	a rosary made up of 108 beads, usually made from wood.
mandir	a Hindu temple or shrine.
mantra	a sacred syllable, word or prayer, usually repeated when recited.

moksha	final freedom from the cycle of birth, death and rebirth.
murti	image of a deity, used as a focus for worship.
Om	the sacred symbol representing God, the Supreme Being.
pandit	a learned man, usually a brahmin.
prashād	food such as fruit, nuts and sweets which is offered to deities and shared by Hindus after worship.
pūjā	an act of worship performed at home at the family shrine or in a mandir.
pūjāri	a brahmin who conducts puja in a mandir and advises families in religious matters.
samsāra	life in the world as a cycle of birth, death and rebirth.
samskāra	sacrament; life-cycle ritual.
Sanātan dharma	'eternal' or 'ageless' religion; a term used by Hindus for 'Hinduism'.
satsang	a gathering for devotional singing and worship.
shruti	'that which is heard'; scriptures 'revealed' by God.
smriti	'that which is remembered'; scriptures based on traditions.
tilak	a mark made of kum kum and put on a worshipper's forehead. It is a sign of respect and blessing.
varna	'colour'. Ancient Hindu society was divided into four varnas – groups.

Book List

Manju Aggarwal and Chris Fairclough, *I am a Hindu*, Watts Books, 1984

Liz Aylett, *Seeking Religion: The Hindu Experience*, Hodder and Stoughton, 1995

Debjani Chatterjee, *The Elephant-Headed God and Other Hindu Tales*, Lutterworth Press, 1989 (Twelve stories of Hindu gods and goddesses, retold from some of the main Hindu scriptures.)

W. Owen Cole, *Meeting Hinduism*, Longman, 1987

Jacqueline Hirst with Geeta Pandy, *Growing up in Hinduism*, Longman, 1990 (Presents a child's–eye view of what it means to be a Hindu and also includes suggestions for activities.)

Robert Jackson and Eleanor Nesbitt, *Listening to Hindus*, Unwin Hyman, 1990 (an informative book about some main Hindu beliefs and practices. Hindus of all ages describe how their religion is lived out in their everyday lives.)

Madhur Jaffrey, *Seasons of Splendour: Tales, Myths and Legends of India*, Puffin, 1985 (a good collection of stories, in particular connected with festivals.)

Dilip Kadodwala and Paul Gateshill, *Hindu Festivals*, Heinemann, 1995 (an introduction to the main Hindu festivals, as seen through the eyes of Hindu children in Britain.)

V. P. (Hemant) Kanitkar, *Discovering Sacred Texts: Hindu Scriptures*, Heinemann Educational, 1994

V.P. (Hemant) Kanitkar, *Hindu Stories*, Wayland, 1985 (Using the original sources of the Hindu Epics, the author retells some stories of Rama and Krishna. Suitable for younger children.)

Note on Dates

Each religion has its own system for counting the years of its history. The starting point may be related to the birth or death of a special person or an important event. In everyday life, today, when different communities have dealings with each other, they need to use the same counting system for setting dates in the future and writing accounts of the past. The Western system is now used throughout the world. It is based on Christian beliefs about Jesus: AD (Anno Domini = in the year of our Lord) and BC (Before Christ). Members of the various world faiths use the common Western system, but, instead of AD and BC, they say and write CE (in the Common Era) and BCE (before the Common Era).

Index